Watch it Grow

A Frog's Life

Nancy Dickmann

www.raintreepublishers.co.uk
Visit our website to find out
more information about
Raintree books.

To order:

☎ Phone 0845 6044371

🖷 Fax +44 (0) 1865 312263

🖳 Email myorders@raintreepublishers.co.uk

Customers from outside the UK please telephone +44 1865 312262

Raintree is an imprint of Capstone Global Library Limited,
a company incorporated in England and Wales having its
registered office at 7 Pilgrim Street, London, EC4V 6LB
– Registered company number: 6695582

Text © Capstone Global Library Limited 2010
First published in hardback in 2010
The moral rights of the proprietor have been asserted.

Edited by Nancy Dickmann, Rebecca Rissman, and Catherine Veitch
Designed by Joanna Hinton-Malivoire
Picture research by Mica Brancic
Production by Victoria Fitzgerald
Originated by Capstone Global Library Ltd
Printed and bound in China by South China Printing
Company Ltd

ISBN 978 0 431 19533 9
14 13 12 11 10
10 9 8 7 6 5 4 3 2 1

British Library Cataloguing in Publication Data
Dickmann, Nancy.
Frog. -- (Watch it grow)
571.8'1789-dc22

Acknowledgements
We would would like to thank the following for permission to reproduce
photographs: Getty Images p. **6** (© Dorling Kindersley/Neil Fletcher);
iStockphoto pp. **8** (© Robert Ellis), **9** (© Sven Peter), **14** (Tommounsey),
20 (© Alan Crawford), **21** (© Jerry Whaley), **22 top** (© Sven Peter);
Photolibrary pp. **4** (age fotostock/Caroline Commins), **10** (White/
© Rosemary Calvert), **11** (© Eric Anthony Johnson), **13** (Animals Animals/
© Zigmund Leszczynski), **15** (Animals Animals/© Zigmund Leszczynski),
17 (Oxford Scientific (OSF)/© Berndt Fischer), **18** (Oxford Scientific
(OSF)/© Paulo de Oliveira), **19** (Oxford Scientific (OSF)/© David Maitland),
22 right (White/© Rosemary Calvert), **22 bottom** (Animals Animals/
© Zigmund Leszczynski), **23 top** (White/© Rosemary Calvert); Shutterstock
pp. **5** (© Steve McWilliam), **7** (© Katharina Wittfeld), **12** (© Wolfgang
Staib), **16** (efiplus), **22 left** (efiplus), **23 middle** (2happy), **23 bottom**
(© Wolfgang Staib).

Front cover photograph (main) of a common frog reproduced with
permission of Shutterstock (© Steve McWilliam). Front cover photograph
(inset) of a close-up of frogspawn reproduced with permission of
iStockphoto (© Robert Ellis). Back cover photograph of a frog and
frogspawn reproduced with permission of iStockphoto (© Robert Ellis).

The publisher would like to thank Nancy Harris for her assistance in the
preparation of this book.

Every effort has been made to contact copyright holders of material
reproduced in this book. Any omissions will be rectified in subsequent
printings if notice is given to the publisher.

Contents

Life cycles

All living things have a life cycle.

Frogs have a life cycle.

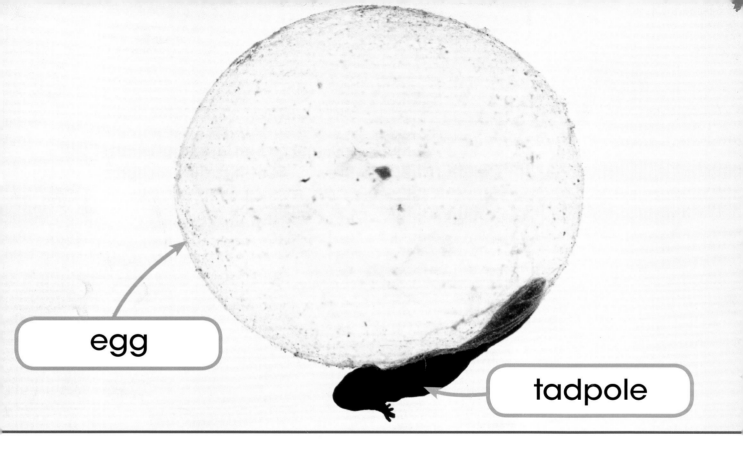

egg

tadpole

A tadpole hatches from an egg.

It grows into a frog.

eggs

A frog lays eggs.
Later it will die.

Eggs

frogspawn

A female frog lays eggs in a pond.
The eggs are called frogspawn.

tadpole

Each egg has a tadpole inside.

Tadpoles

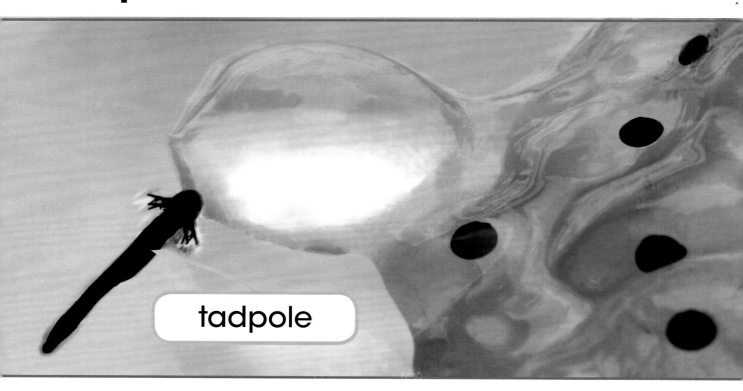

tadpole

A tadpole hatches from the egg.

tail

A tadpole has a tail.

Growing and changing

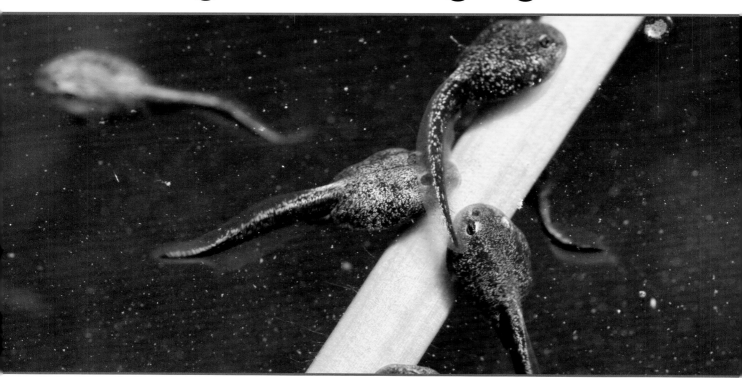

The tadpole lives in a pond.

The tadpole eats plants to grow.

legs

Soon the tadpole starts to grow legs.

Soon the tadpole has four legs.

Becoming a frog

The tadpole grows into a frog.

legs

When the frog is grown it uses its strong legs to jump.

tongue

The frog catches insects with
its tongue.

The frog also eats worms
and spiders.

eggs

A female frog lays eggs in a pond.

The life cycle starts again.

Life cycle of a frog

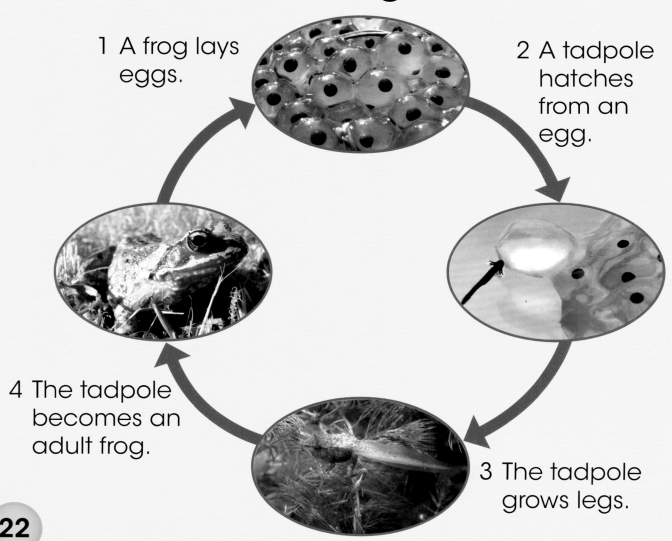

1 A frog lays eggs.

2 A tadpole hatches from an egg.

4 The tadpole becomes an adult frog.

3 The tadpole grows legs.

22

Picture glossary

 hatch to be born from an egg

 insect very small creature with six legs

 tadpole young frog

Index

Notes to parents and teachers

Before reading

Ask the children if they know what a baby dog is called. Then see if they can name a baby cat, horse, cow, sheep, and pig. Do they know what a baby frog is called? Talk about how some animal babies look like small versions of the adults and some animal babies look very different.

After reading

• In the spring you could try hatching some tadpoles. Put a little frogspawn in a tank with the pondwater kept between 15°C and 20°C. Add pondweed to the tank for the tadpoles to eat when they hatch. You can also feed them with lettuce leaves. Get the children to record any changes they see to the tadpoles each day. When the tadpoles grow legs, make sure there are stones in the tank that come above the water so the young frogs can climb up and breathe. Release the fully-grown frogs together near a clean pond.

• Get the children to dance the lifecycle of a frog. Start with them curled up tight, huddled up close together like frogspawn. Get them to "hatch" one by one and move around the room as if they are swimming like tadpoles. Finally tell them to hop around the room like frogs. You could play some music for them to dance to, for example Paul McCartney's "Frog Chorus".